Why Are Resources Important?

 HOUGHTON MIFFLIN HARCOURT

Printed in Mexico

ISBN: 978-0-544-07252-7

7 8 9 10 0908 20 19 18 17 16

4500607981   A B C D E F G

Be an Active Reader!

 Look at these words.

natural resource	salt water
human-made resource	conserve
rock	reuse
weathering	reduce
glacier	recycle
fresh water	dispose

 Look for answers to these questions.

Why are resources important to us?

What are different kinds of resources?

What can we learn about rocks?

Where does our water come from?

How can we take care of our resources?

Why are resources important to us?

Are you sitting at a desk? What is on your desk? How do you use your desk? How do you use the items on your desk?

Your desk and the items on it are resources. A resource is anything people use to meet their needs. Resources help us every day. We use them at home and at school. We use resources outside, too.

These computers are made of resources like metal and plastic.

What are different kinds of resources?

Resources are all around us. But not all resources are the same.

Some resources come from nature. A natural resource is anything from nature that people can use. Water, rocks, sunlight, trees, and animals are all natural resources.

Some natural resources are living. Some are nonliving. Trees are living resources. Water is a nonliving resource.

People can use wood from trees to build houses.

Steel and plastic in cars are human-made resources.

Other important resources do not come from nature. A human-made resource is something made by humans for people to use.

You use things made from human-made resources all the time. You ride in cars made of steel and plastic. Steel and plastic are human-made resourses

A geologist is a scientist who studies rocks.

What can we learn about rocks?

A rock is a hard, nonliving object from the ground. Rocks are made of many different minerals. Different minerals make different kinds of rocks. These minerals form rocks in different ways, too. Minerals give rocks their different textures and colors.

Rocks are important natural resources. People use rocks in many ways. Builders use large rocks to build stone walls or houses.

Artists carve rocks into small shapes or large statues. This kind of art is called sculpture. Some artists use rocks to make jewelry.

Over time, wind and weather break down rocks into small pieces. This change is called weathering.

Artists carved these faces into rock at Mount Rushmore.

Where does our water come from?

Water is everywhere on Earth. Most of the water on Earth is found in the oceans. Rivers, lakes, and glaciers hold water, too. A glacier is a large thick sheet of slow-moving ice. You can find glaciers in very cold places, such as Alaska.

Earth's water flows underground between rocks. It often fills the spaces around rocks and sand. Water in the air forms clouds.

This glacier contains frozen fresh water.

A lake has land all around it.

lake

There are two kinds of water. Fresh water has very little salt. Rivers, most lakes, glaciers, and small ponds contain fresh water. The water in a lake does not flow. But the fresh water in rivers does flow.

Salt water is much saltier than fresh water. Most salt water is found in oceans and seas.

How can we take care of our resources?

To take care of our natural resources, we must conserve them. That means we have to use things wisely so they last longer.

There are three ways to conserve: reuse, reduce, and recycle. When you reuse something, you use it again. You can also reduce, or use less of something.

You can conserve by reusing shopping bags.

How else can you conserve resources? Many cities recycle old materials to make new things. Old newspapers can be made into school notebooks. Glass jars or bottles can be made into windows.

Some things cannot be used again or recycled. You must dispose, or get rid, of them. Always throw your trash in a trashcan. Never toss it on the street.

Recycling center

Many objects made from glass, paper, metal, or plastic can be recycled.

Responding

Make a Poster

Work with a partner. Make a poster about conserving resources. Explain how to reduce, reuse, and recycle. Tell your classmates about your poster.

Write a Paragraph

Write a paragraph about a natural resource and a human-made resource that you use every day. Explain what each resource is and why it is important to you. Read your paragraph in class.